Mammoth Bones
—and—
Broken Stones

The Mystery of North America's First People

David L. Harrison

With Illustrations by Richard Hilliard
and Archaeological Photographs

Boyds Mills Press
Honesdale, Pennsylvania

Acknowledgments

My sincere thanks go to Neal Lopinot, Ph.D., director of the Center for Archaeological Research, Missouri State University, for reading the manuscript, offering suggestions, and introducing me to other important figures in this field.

Many others helped as well, including Jack H. Ray, research archaeologist, Center for Archaeological Research, Missouri State University; Kary Stackelbeck, Ph.D., Department of Anthropology, University of Kentucky; and Juliet E. Morrow, Ph.D., station archaeologist, Arkansas Archaeological Survey, and associate professor, University of Arkansas, by reading the manuscript and providing valuable insights.

The following people also made this a better book with their instructive comments or unique photographs from many of the sites described: Anthony T. Boldurian, Ph.D., professor of anthropology, University of Pittsburgh; Joanne Dickenson, Ph.D., on-site curator of Blackwater Draw Museum, Eastern New Mexico University; John Montgomery, Ph.D., director of Blackwater Draw Museum, Eastern New Mexico University; Tom D. Dillehay, Ph.D., Department of Anthropology, Vanderbilt University; Albert C. Goodyear, Ph.D., director of the Allendale Paleoindian Expedition, South Carolina Institute of Archaeology and Anthropology, University of South Carolina; Michael B. Collins, Ph.D., Texas Archaeological Research Laboratory, University of Texas at Austin; Scott Hootman, cave specialist and stone-point collector; and Kristine Paulus, assistant archivist, University of Pennsylvania Museum of Archaeology and Anthropology.

I am grateful to the following educators and their students for reading the manuscript and improving it with their comments: Bela Kletnick, literacy coach at P.S. 86, Bronx, New York, and her fifth- and sixth-grade students; Denise Fredrick, Ph.D., former science curriculum coordinator, Springfield Public Schools, Springfield, Missouri; Christie Harr, Reading Recovery teacher-leader, Springfield Public Schools, Springfield, Missouri; Julie Strickland, adjunct professor, Brewton Park College, and former elementary-school librarian, Moultrie, Georgia; Kathy Holderith, affiliate faculty member, Regis College and former third-grade teacher, Littleton, Colorado; Jennifer Harrison, fourth-grade teacher, Beaverton, Oregon; and Liz Biller, middle-school and high-school teacher, La Quinta, California.

—David L. Harrison

CONTENTS

WHO ARE WE LOOKING FOR?

Clues for the Future

MORE THAN FOUR THOUSAND YEARS AGO, a man sat on a riverbank holding a thin piece of flintlike rock called chert. Using the tip of a deer antler, he chipped flakes off the rock to fashion a point at one end. He made the edges sharp enough to pierce tough hide and rip through muscle.

It didn't take the man long to do this. He had done it many times. If he made a mistake or the point broke, he tossed it aside and picked up another rock.

Seven centuries after the hunter sat on the riverbank, King Tut would rule Egypt. The village that would grow into Paris, France, was still two thousand years into the future. It would be another two thousand years after that before a man walking along the river would find the hunter's spearpoint. By then this place would be called Big Eddy. The stream would be known as the Sac River in Missouri.

Clues from our ancient past are hard to find.

Archaeologists Neal Lopinot and Jack Ray

Big Eddy beside the Sac River

Neal Lopinot and Jack Ray are archaeologists (scientists who study ancient human cultures). Like many archaeologists, they are interested in learning more about the earliest people to reach North America.

In 1996 Neal and Jack came to the Sac River to visit Big Eddy. For many years local collectors had been finding stone points along the bank. While Neil and Jack were there, Jack studied the bank close to the water and spotted some rocks sticking out of a thin layer of soil ten feet below the top. These were no ordinary rocks. They had been shaped by human hands. The scientists agreed to return the following summer with a team. They would dig below the surface to see what might be buried there. Both men were excited when they left. Waiting for next summer was going to be hard.

There was little time to spare. Currents caused by the dam upstream nibbled away nearly two feet of the bank each year. Before much longer, any secrets buried at Big Eddy would be lost forever under the invading water of the Sac River.

Quest for the First People to Arrive in North America

Humans belong to the animal kingdom and are known as *Homo sapiens*. Discoveries of fossil skulls and bones in East Africa show that the first of our kind developed there in the open grasslands around two hundred thousand years ago. Soon after that our voice box (larynx) changed so that humans could develop the ability to speak.

By one hundred thousand years ago, people looked much like we do today. Around that time, *Homo sapiens* began to migrate, moving north out of Africa. Signs of them have been found in Europe and Asia. By fifty thousand to forty thousand years ago, humans made it south to Australia.

North and South America were the last continents to be settled. Who were the first people here? How did they get here? When?

The trail is cold and North America is huge. The combined countries of India, Saudi Arabia, Egypt, France, Spain, Iraq, Japan, Germany, Italy, England, Greece, North Korea, South Korea, Denmark, and Israel could fit inside our continent.

In such a vast area, where do we look for signs thousands of years old of the first people? Traces of them lie in caves, buried in the earth, or even beneath the sea. Discovering positive evidence is rare and hard to prove. What seem like clues often turn into tantalizing riddles with more than one possible answer. Was this rock chipped by a hunter or under the foot of a passing mammoth? What produced this fragment of charcoal—a campfire or a forest fire? Whose mouth sucked the marrow from this cracked bone?

The search for our past is a story of many stories. Some will surprise you.

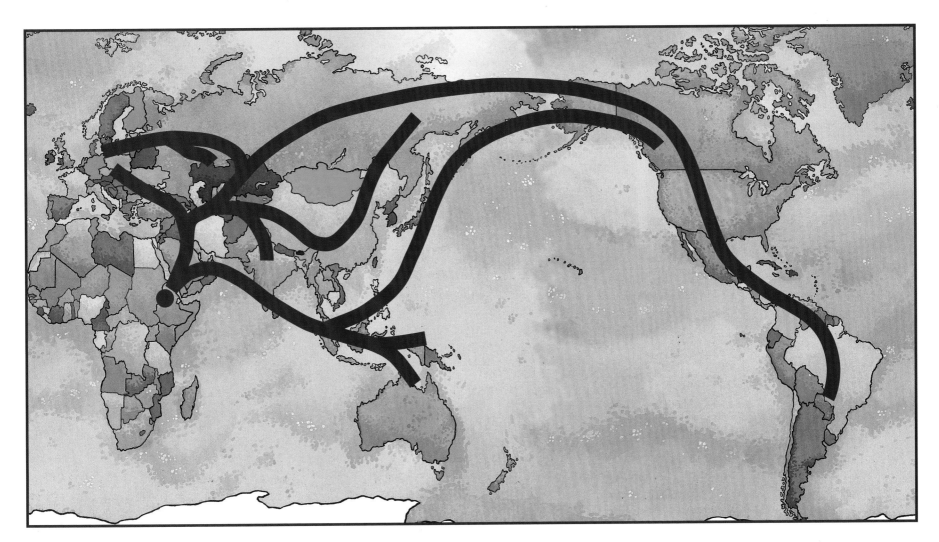

Human migration routes out of Africa

Nature Provides a Bridge 2

A Time of Snow and Ice

WE LIVE IN WHAT GEOLOGISTS CALL THE
Holocene (HOL-uh-seen) period. The period before this,
the Pleistocene (PLY-stah-seen), ended roughly twelve thousand
years ago at the end of the last ice age.

Earth passes through one complete ice age cycle roughly
every one hundred thousand years. Ice ages are caused by three
other cycles: the longest and shortest distances Earth orbits
around the sun, the changing tilt of Earth toward or away from
the sun, and the way Earth slowly "wobbles" back and forth as it
moves in orbit. Together these are called the Milankovitch cycles.
Milutin Milankovitch was a Serbian mathematician who explained
how the cycles cause the great northern ice caps to grow and
shrink at regular intervals.

Ice age mammoths on the move

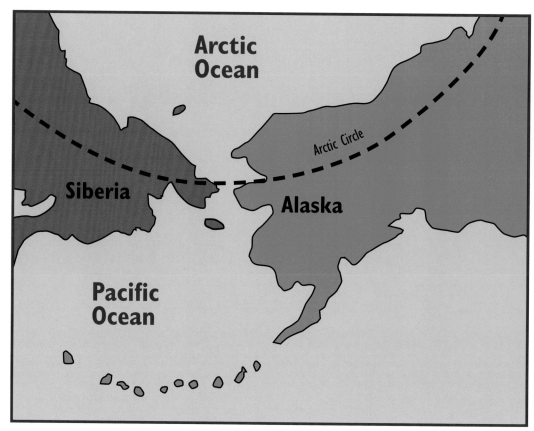

Siberia and Alaska separated by the Bering Strait

At the coldest end of ice age cycles (also called glacials), summer temperatures become too cool to melt all of the winter snows. Over thousands of years, snow continues to build up until it turns into sheets of ice as much as two miles thick. These vast fields of ice eventually cover much of northern North America, Europe, and parts of Asia. About twenty thousand years ago, the North American ice fields reached as far south as Missouri.

Our planet's water is usually recycled. It evaporates from the ocean and much of it falls on land as rain or snow. Most water is eventually carried back to the ocean in rivers and underground streams. The cycle keeps repeating itself.

During glacial periods, so much water is captured as ice and snow that the cycle is interrupted. With less water being returned to the ocean, sea levels around the world begin to fall. New land is exposed for as much as two hundred miles offshore.

A Land Called Beringia

When sea levels drop enough, sometimes newly exposed land forms a bridge that connects one continent to another. For example, more than once over the past two million years, western Alaska and eastern Asia (Siberia) were joined by land. This region was the flat floor of two seas, the Bering and the Chukchi (chook-CHEE), until the falling waters drained away and exposed the sea floor as land. During the most recent glacial (ice age), the land bridge was one thousand miles wide and twice the size of Texas. Today it is known as Beringia (beh-REN-gee-ah).

Toward the end of the last glacial, most of the ice had melted, so ocean levels rose until water once again flowed over the region. Today eastern Asia and western Alaska are divided by a narrow strip of sea called the Bering Strait.

To learn about the ancient, sunken land bridge of Beringia, scientists study fossils found on both sides of the Bering Strait. Many of the same species of animals, such as bison, caribou, and mammoths, once lived in both places so we know that they crossed from one continent to the other. We know what the grazing animals liked to eat, which tells us what sorts of plants grew in Beringia. Knowing about the plants gives us clues about climate and soil conditions.

And how do the earliest people to reach North America fit into the picture? Looking for the answers takes detective work at its best. Anthropologists study human societies and cultures. Archaeologists seek physical evidence of human activities. Other scientists study hereditary traits, languages, soil, plants, animals, glaciers, weather, and even parasites. Clue by clue, glimpses emerge of times, places, and life long, long ago.

Siberia and Alaska connected by the land bridge called Beringia

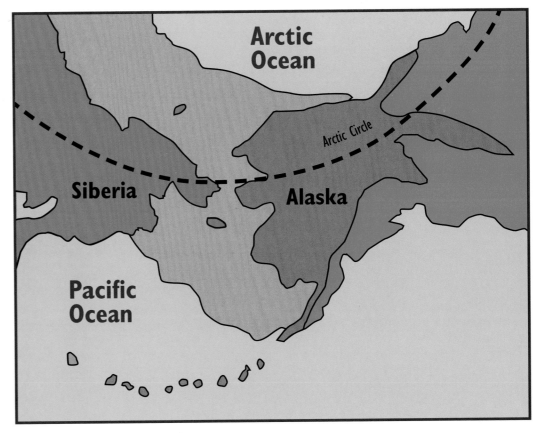

THE MYSTERIOUS CLOVIS CULTURE

Last Ones across the Bridge

BERINGIA WAS PROBABLY WINDY AND DISAGREEABLE.
Poplars in scattered groves were among the few trees that could
survive. Although the climate was too dry for the great ice sheets
to form there, areas may have been dotted and crossed with icy
lakes and rivers. Studies of ancient pollen and seeds show the
kinds of grasses and herbs that grew there. One was a blue-flowered
plant called arctic lupine. A ten-thousand-year-old lemming nest
found in Alaska contained frozen seeds of arctic lupine. When the
ice age seeds were planted, they grew!

Creatures of all sizes may have grazed and stalked their
way across Beringia—moving from the freezing temperatures
of Siberia in Asia toward the slightly warmer conditions of
Alaska. Some migrated the other way. Lemmings, voles, shrews,
and ground squirrels scurried through the low growth where
mammoths towered fourteen feet above them. Bison and musk-ox
depended on heavy coats against the biting winds of winter.

Mammoths, caribou, and bison grazing on the tundra of Beringia

A lineup of fierce predators would have stalked the grazers. Massive, short-faced bears could sprint like horses. Saber-tooth cats plunged fangs like daggers into their victims' throats. Lions nine feet long leaped from ambush. Dire wolves with crushing jaws crunched through flesh and bone.

The smartest and most cunning of all predators would be present, too: humans. Ice age hunters had no plans to go anywhere in particular. Life itself was a long, dangerous journey. As humans gradually made their way eastward following the migrating herds, people would die along the way and babies would be born. Generations would pass. Small groups paused when hunting was good and then pushed on. Traveling over land in summer and ice in winter, some of those roving bands are thought to have eventually reached North America.

Heading South

Twenty thousand years ago, most of Canada and the northern United States lay under two immense sheets of ice. The Cordilleran (cor-dill-YAIR-en) sheet stretched from the Rocky Mountains westward to the Pacific Ocean. The Laurentide ice sheet extended eastward to the Atlantic.

Scientists think that these ice fields sometimes grew together and at other periods moved apart, leaving an ice-free corridor between them along the eastern slopes of the Rocky Mountains.

Near the end of the last glacial, enough melting had occurred that the borders of the Cordilleran and Laurentide sheets separated permanently.

For a long time after the shrinking ice sheets drew apart,

Archaeologist Edgar Howard searches for the presence of early humans at Blackwater Draw, New Mexico, 1933

The way it might have looked thirteen thousand years ago at Blackwater Draw

the land between them must have been a nightmare of frozen soil, bogs and marshes, frigid lakes, and rampaging rivers. So much ice nearby would create freezing winds. Little vegetation could grow. Grazing animals couldn't survive. Without food, neither could humans.

But as summer temperatures continued to rise, more melting occurred until eventually grasses sprouted once again. It was finally possible for grazing herds (and humans) to migrate south along the twelve-hundred-mile route to the Great Plains of the United States.

Imagine children finding ways to entertain themselves. Maybe they gathered dried bison dung for the fires or killed ground squirrels with rocks to help feed their families. Mothers would bundle babies in furs and carry them close to their bodies. Adults would stay alert for the possibility of food or signs of danger. In their world, hunters could quickly become the hunted.

Bagging a Mammoth

Here is something else to imagine. The hunters in your band have just killed a young mammoth! One of their stone-tipped spears pierced the creature's thick hide and found its heart. As the raging sixteen-thousand-pound mother lunged to trample the men, the juvenile crumpled to the ground. This was noisy and exciting and dangerous.

Your people will feast for days. Some of the remaining meat will be dried to take with you when you leave. Elders will retell stories around the fire while men and women fashion new tools from bone, wood, ivory, and antler.

Women will gather plants for medicine and weaving. Footwear will be repaired. Clothes will be made or mended, sewn together with strong plant fibers or thin strips of leather.

Thousands of years from now, a young man will visit this place. He will find stone points and mammoth bones from your feast. Your people will become famous. You and your people will even have a special name: Clovis.

In 1906 in the territory that would become the state of New Mexico six years later, the daughter of a railroad man won the honor of picking a new name for the tiny railroad settlement of Riley's Switch. She chose Clovis, after an ancient king. Twenty-three years later, in 1929, nineteen-year-old James Ridgley Whiteman was fossil hunting in Blackwater Draw, an ancient river valley south of Clovis.

This is a hot, rocky area whose sandy soil is dotted with sagebrush and spiked with cactus plants. Ridgley knew the place well. When he found stone points mixed with fossil animal bones, he reported his discovery.

During the years that followed, teams of archaeologists came to investigate what Ridgley had found. The early humans who left their traces there were probably very efficient at killing small game and living off the land, but judging by the size of their stone points and the animal bones uncovered at the site, they must have hunted big game, too.

The scientists named these mystery people Clovis. That's much better than Riley's Switch. Thank goodness for the railroad man's daughter!

James Ridgley Whiteman at Blackwater Draw, New Mexico, 1929

Were Clovis the First People?

Clovis points are easy to recognize. The maker flaked chips off both sides of a thin piece of rock to form sharp edges leading to a point. A groove (called a flute) was chipped from the base so it would fit into the end of a shaft to make a spear.

Clovis points have been discovered in hundreds of places across North America and in all but five states. Mammoth bones have been found at more than twelve of the sites. Whoever these hunters were, they were aggressive. Their

Clovis stone knife (top) and two points found with mammoth bones at Blackwater Draw

largest points are longer than a man's hand. One found in Washington measures 9¾ inches long.

In 1947 a chemist named Willard Libby developed a test called radiocarbon (or carbon-14) dating to determine the age of plants and animals that lived in the past. C-14 years are slightly longer than regular calendar years. (In this book, ages are expressed in calendar years.) Using C-14 dating, some scientists believe that the Clovis culture flourished for about two hundred years—from roughly 11,050 to 10,800 C-14 years ago, which is about 13,125 to 12,925 calendar-years ago. Some scientists believe the Clovis culture began hundreds of years earlier.

Clovis point, larger than a man's hand

Did Others Get Here First? 4

Questioning the Clovis First Idea

WHEN CLOVIS WAS FIRST DISCOVERED,
it was the earliest-known record of people on this continent.
Many archaeologists concluded that Clovis represented the first
humans to reach North America. The idea became known as
Clovis First.

But not everyone agreed with the Clovis First idea. Not all
the pieces seemed to fit. Some studies of ancient pollen show
that although grass and other edible plants grew in Beringia, they
may not have flourished everywhere. Instead of endless supplies
of plants for grazing animals, meadows may have been small and
too scattered to support major herds. Fewer grazers would mean
fewer predators, including humans. Therefore, maybe the
land bridge was not the best route to North America, or the first.

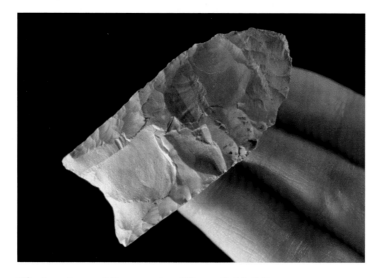

Clovis point at Martens site, Chesterfield, Missouri

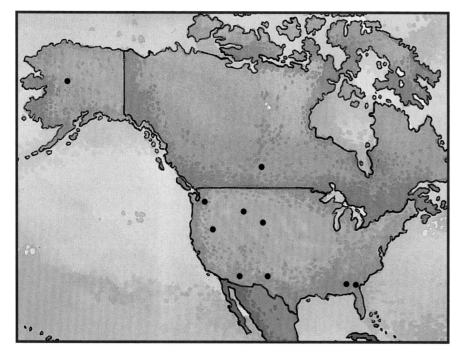

Locations of many reported Clovis sites

Also, by the time Clovis showed up in what is now New Mexico, they had perfected their enormous spearpoints. If they had developed this skill during a long migration from Asia across Beringia, shouldn't a few early versions have turned up along their route?

Where Is the Missing Link?

No "missing-link" Clovis points have been found in Asia, Alaska, Canada, or anywhere else in North America, at least that we recognize.

At a place in central Alaska called Moose Creek, a group known as Nenana (ni-NAH-nuh) was making stone points three hundred years before Clovis. However, their points were shaped differently and not made in the same way as those by Clovis. Some scientists have wondered if Nenana could be the missing link, but most have not accepted that idea.

In a few hundred years the Clovis culture spread across North America from coast to coast plus what is now Canada, Mexico, and Venezuela. Many archaeologists have questioned how people on foot could crisscross millions of square miles that fast.

Life Thirteen Thousand Years Ago

In those long-ago days, bands of roving humans would be small, probably no more than thirty or forty, including women, children, and babies. Picture such a group. A few women are pregnant or carrying small children. Some of the elders suffer from arthritis or injuries and move slowly. Over the horizon in every direction stretches the unknown. In their constant search for food, these people will encounter deserts, rivers, canyons, mountains, prairies, forests, swamps, and marshes.

They know how to hunt big game, but mammoths don't come along every day. Some experts wonder if Clovis-age hunters killed so many mammoths that the species became extinct. Other scientists believe the mammoths perished because of changing weather patterns and loss of the right kinds of plants to eat. A new theory under debate is that an asteroid three miles wide struck or exploded above the ice cap over Canada 12,900 years ago, near the end of the last ice age. According to the theory, this caused a firestorm of deadly flying debris and triggered thirteen hundred years of cooler temperatures. Beginning with this period, thirty-five to forty species of big-game animals associated with Clovis died out.

New Ideas about Clovis

In the time of Clovis, we might guess that people lived according to the seasons and the animals they followed. When the hunters got lucky, the group relaxed and enjoyed fresh meat. When there was plenty of game in the area, why move on? The men made shelters using saplings, branches, grasses, animal skins, and whatever else served the purpose. If the band discovered an inviting cave, maybe they camped there for a while.

Seeing other humans would surely be rare. Now and then two groups might meet by chance. More likely, bands came together every few months or years at prearranged places to

Clovis hunted bison for fresh meat.

Michael Collins

The site at Gault, Texas

exchange news and choose mates. Mostly these rugged people were on their own to deal with injuries, illness, death, storms, floods, and forest fires. Harsh winters forced them to hole up and wait for better times.

Clues at Gault, Texas

Intriguing clues to the Clovis mystery lie in a small, spring-fed valley in central Texas. An important feature of the place, called Gault, is an endless supply of chert, the best kind of rock for making stone tools. It is also a huge Clovis site. In an area a half-mile long and 650 feet wide, early humans visited and sometimes stayed for long periods.

Since 1998 a team of scientists led by Michael Collins has investigated Gault. From a small sampling of the site they have already recovered one million pieces of stone, bone, and teeth from the Clovis era.

Many other known Clovis sites were temporary camps where parties paused long enough only to make weapons or butcher their kill. (That's why our early ideas about Clovis were of roving bands of hunters set on bagging big game and moving on.) Gault appears to present a different picture. Many tools found at Gault seem fitted for digging, cutting grass, and working with wood. These humans hunted small animals as well as big ones. Could there have been more than one kind of Clovis people?

Debating Tough Questions

For about seventy years, the belief that Clovis came first was so strong that some archaeologists resisted other possibilities. Yet suspected traces of more ancient humans kept turning up. One by one, new ideas and evidence were debated.

What if humans were already here before Clovis, widely scattered across the continent and well established? Maybe they didn't even all speak the same language.

What if Clovis was not a single tribe or nation of people but merely a special technique of working with stone? In that case we would not be talking about the Clovis people. We would be talking about the Clovis method for making stone weapons and tools.

Whoever developed those newfangled stone points, it didn't take long for the news to spread. The most advanced technology of the day—the Clovis point—was handed around from group to group. It was the best thing yet for bringing down big game, cutting meat, scraping hides, and even sawing through tough plant stalks. Who wouldn't want to have the latest all-purpose tool?

If earlier people (pre-Clovis) were already here, who were they? They were certainly clever pioneers who made everything they needed. Unfortunately, we have little evidence to study. Nearly all of the materials they used except stone rotted away thousands of years ago.

Stone spears and knives make us think of hulking brutes swarming over a mammoth or battling a giant bear. But these people were neither dumb nor brutish. From the fossil record of humans found on other continents, we know that thousands of years before Clovis humans already had large brains like ours today. In many ways they probably looked a lot like we would after a few weeks at camp.

Believing that people reached North America before Clovis makes sense to a lot of scientists. But finding positive proof of their presence is very difficult. One reason is that no one knows exactly what to look for.

Archaeologists at work at Gault, Texas

Excavating takes skill and patience.

Clovis points found at Gault

PROVING THE CLUES ARE RIGHT 5

The Strict Rules of Archaeology

MANY SITES SEEM AT FIRST TO HOLD
important artifacts (something made and left by humans).
On closer examination, some of these turn out to be created by
nature. To help decide between real evidence and false alarms,
archaeologists have created tough standards that must be met.
Here are three of them.

One: Establish that the artifact was made by a human.
Archaeologists Neal Lopinot and Jack Ray dug a trench and filled
it with small rocks. They arranged for adult Indian elephants
from a zoo to walk over the rocks as mastodons might have done
thousands of years ago.

How can we know which artifacts were made by humans and which were made by nature?

The elephants' great weight broke one rock out of every twenty. The breaks did not produce anything like finished points, but some left chips and sharp edges that might be mistaken as evidence of stone craftsmen at work. This is why archaeologists always look for other signs of human activity when they find what could be clues from our ancient past.

Two: Establish when the artifact existed. Carbon-14 testing doesn't work on stone, but it does on bone. If a stone point is found with a mammoth bone and the bone's age can

Using elephants, scientists attempt to determine the difference between human-made artifacts and those made my nature.

be dated, does that mean that the point existed at the same time? A rodent could have dug a tunnel and the point might have slipped down the tunnel and landed near the bone buried below. Researchers study the soil to make certain that nothing has disturbed it.

Three: Establish that the site shows no signs of erosion, which might rearrange the layers of soil, or flooding of ancient rivers that could carry bones and artifacts from one area to another. Large quantities of fossil bison bones were found near the Bering Strait. Does this show that herds once roamed the area? It might, but another possibility is that bones scattered along ancient riverbanks washed downstream over time until they gradually built up in one area.

Because of these demanding requirements, archaeologists retest and double-check suspected evidence before they will agree that they have found another real piece of our past. This is how science works. No one has all the answers, but many people working on the same problem slowly add to what we know.

Real artifact discovered at Gault

False artifacts made by elephants

GLIMPSES OF OUR DEEP PAST  6

Was Someone at Gault before Clovis?

MORE THAN ONE-THIRD OF ALL CLOVIS
artifacts excavated so far have come from the Gault site in central
Texas. However, below all the Clovis evidence, the team discovered
something else—ancient animal remains and chipped stone tools,
which are different from Clovis.

Something else was different, too: fire-cracked rocks. At
Clovis sites, fire pits were lined and surrounded by stones so
the hottest stones seldom cracked. The presence of fire-cracked
rocks could be evidence of more primitive fire building skills. Did
someone live at Gault before Clovis?

Archaeologist Mike Collins cautions against assuming that
these differences are absolute proof of an older culture. But when
we add these findings to those that have turned up at other sites, it
is hard to ignore the possibilities.

What secrets would Meadowcroft Rockshelter hold?

Back to the Man on the Riverbank

We never know when or where the next clues will be discovered. For example, at Missouri's Big Eddy site the team led by Neal Lopinot and Jack Ray dug below the place where the man on the riverbank fashioned a stone point four thousand years ago.

Seven feet down, the researchers uncovered a spot where someone else made a point thousands of years earlier. Chips from his work lay in a pattern, probably between his legs where he sat. A broken point was found in clay that dated 12,700 years old.

But that wasn't the only surprise buried in the bank along the Sac River. Lower still, in clay 14,500 years old, a broken forty-pound boulder possibly used as an anvil was found. How was the boulder broken unless by humans? The researchers also uncovered a hand-size, sharp-edged flake of chert; two fist-size stones sitting upright side by side; and a large bone fragment possibly from a butchered bison.

These signs suggest that people were in southwest Missouri before Clovis. Decisive proof could be inches away.

The Mystery at Monte Verde, Chile

Not all of the clues to our past are found in North America. In the South American country of Chile in 1976, a university student of archaeologist Tom Dillehay's brought him some mastodon bones from a creek bank.

The bones bore curious scratches. Did animals make them? Or could they have been caused during butchering?

Monte Verde, Chile

Mastodons have been extinct for twelve thousand years. Tom decided to check it out.

The place, called Monte Verde, is thirty-six miles from the Pacific Ocean and about that far from the mountains behind it. Sometime in the deep past, a small settlement was there. For more than ten years, Tom and dozens of other researchers investigated Monte Verde. What may have been a bustling community of perhaps twenty to thirty people lay buried in boggy earth, which helped preserve signs that are usually lost, including what appeared to be human footprints!

Based on reports from Monte Verde, these early South Americans apparently cut trees and fashioned planks to frame their main lodge, which they covered with animal hides. They dined on mastodon when they could, but mostly they ate llamas, clams, small animals, wild potatoes, berries,

Ancient footprint at Monte Verde, Chile?

Foundations at Monte Verde, Chile

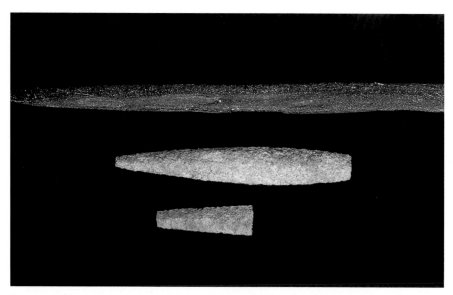

Drill (top) and projectile points from Monte Verde, Chile

Campsite at Monte Verde, Chile

seeds, fruits, and water plants. They doctored themselves with more than a dozen kinds of plants. They fashioned tools and weapons from wood, bone, and stone. They wove rope and carried salt from the ocean. These people were well established. They knew how to take care of themselves.

These discoveries were fascinating. But the big surprise was yet to come. Carbon-14 tests indicated that the site could be at least 14,500 years old. If true, then humans reached the southern tip of South America about one thousand years or more before Clovis appeared in North America!

If these weren't Clovis at Monte Verde, who were they? And where—in the world—did they come from?

A Surprise at Meadowcroft Rockshelter

While Tom Dillehay was working at Monte Verde, another archaeologist—James Adovasio—was researching a site in southwestern Pennsylvania. Meadowcroft Rockshelter has an opening forty-nine feet wide and forty-three feet high, recessed twenty feet into a sandstone bluff. It is located near a creek not far from the Ohio River.

In June 1973, when James and his team began digging into the site, the floor was covered with layers of debris, including beer cans left by modern "cave men." Grains of sandstone and rocks from the ceiling had built up over time. Soil and minerals from the hillside had washed in through cracks in the roof.

James didn't expect to find anything startling. But he was wrong. The layers on the floor were more than ten feet deep and revealed an ancient history. Humans had come to Meadowcroft for thousands of years. The record of their presence went back further and further as the team dug down through time.

Excavating in Meadowcroft Rockshelter, Pennsylvania

Archaeologists mark where sediments have built up over the years inside the rockshelter.

Meadowcroft Rockshelter viewed from across the creek

Possible digging stick from Meadowcroft Rockshelter

Basket fragments from Meadowcroft Rockshelter

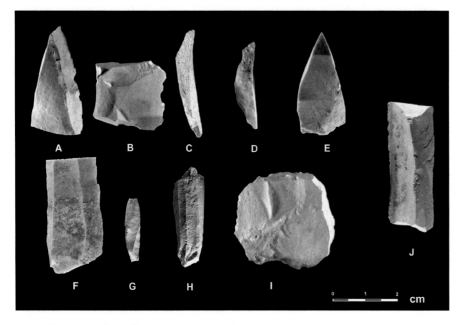

Pre-Clovis artifacts from Topper, South Carolina

At various levels James and his team found fire pits, animal bones, wood tools and utensils, shells, and bits of baskets and cords used for tying or weaving. About two million artifacts and plant and animal remains were eventually recovered from Meadowcroft. It took years to sort them out and make sense of the enormous collection. These early humans were experts at making sophisticated stone tools and weapons. They created spears by inserting rows of sharp stone chips into slots, which were cut into the wood shaft of saplings or limbs cut from trees. These knife-like chips, called microblades, made effective hunting weapons.

When carbon-14 tests came in, James got a surprise like Tom Dillehay's at Monte Verde. Dates associated with the oldest specimens—a small piece of tree bark that might have been part of a basket and bits of charcoal that could have come from a hearth—were at least about eighteen thousand years old. That would place the items more than four thousand years before Clovis hunted mammoths in present-day New Mexico. Were these specimens truly the result of human activity? Some scientists agreed with this interpretation while others did not. This is another example of how archaeologists don't always reach the same conclusions.

The Oldest Dates Yet

Today there are a number of sites in North and South America where possible traces of human life before Clovis have been found. Besides Monte Verde in Chile, Meadowcroft Rockshelter in Pennsylvania, and Gault in Texas, claims have been made for pre-Clovis evidence at sites in Brazil and Oklahoma and two in Virginia (at Cactus Hill and Saltville).

A site called Topper lies near the Savannah River in South Carolina. Since 1998 Al Goodyear has led a team making a series of discoveries with reported dates far earlier than any others so far. About thirteen feet below the ground surface, buried beneath evidence of Clovis culture, Al's team found a variety of stones that they identified as points, blades, and tools made by people who lived before Clovis and whose work does not look like Clovis.

The age of these discoveries was first thought to be twenty thousand to sixteen thousand years, placing them among the oldest possible traces of humans in North America.

Then, on the last day of digging in 2003, the team discovered a layer of charcoal where some of the shaped stones lay. Samples of the charcoal sent for testing turned out to be an astonishing fifty thousand years old. Does such a claim stir up plenty of debate? You bet it does!

Al Goodyear

BOAT PEOPLE 7

What about Boats?

NO MATTER WHEN THE EARLIEST HUMANS
arrived, there is still the question of how they managed to get to
North America. Maybe they did walk across the land bridge, but
Beringia created more than an interior connection between Asia
and Alaska. It also created a long coastline.

The west coast of North America looks much different today
than it did when the ice sheets were at their peak and ocean levels
were at their lowest.

Twenty thousand years ago, the land extended farther out, in
some places as much as fifty miles. Could people who lived by the
sea in Southeast Asia have migrated to North America in skin-
covered boats?

Could early people have come by boat?

Coast Dwellers

There is evidence that by thirty-two thousand years ago humans in Japan were already experienced seafarers. Tools made from volcanic rock were found on an island twenty miles away from the island where the volcano stood. If good sailors kept the shore in sight or moved from island to island, they could travel long distances.

Coast dwellers understood the sea and knew how to live from it. Instead of tracking mammoths and bison, they hunted seals, turtles, and birds. They caught fish, clams, crabs, and sea urchins. They gathered eggs and edible seaweed and picked berries and fruit. They might pause now and then to follow a river upstream or push inland to explore, but they trusted the sea more than the unknown wilderness at their backs.

What if early boat people followed the coastline from Asia to Alaska and from there all the way down the west coast to Central America?

Once they got that far, some groups could turn east and eventually make their way down the Atlantic coast of South America.

Other groups might continue south along the Pacific coast and reach Chile sometime before 14,500 years ago. That might explain how humans arrived at Monte Verde.

To many scientists, it seems logical that early humans moved along the coasts. Any proof that this happened now lies beneath the sea. When the melting glaciers raised sea levels worldwide, all possible human traces along the old shorelines were flooded over.

Stone tool dredged from the sea floor

Looking for a Miracle

It's hard enough to find ancient clues on dry land. How could anyone hope to discover evidence 150 to 450 feet beneath the Pacific Ocean?

Scientists use sonar and dredges. Sonar is a kind of underwater camera that bounces sound waves off the ocean bottom and records how long it takes them to come back.

Using sonar, scientists created images of the sea floor off the coast of British Columbia, Canada, between Queen Charlotte and Vancouver islands. The goal was to discover sunken shorelines that would have been above water during the last ice age.

After a long, patient search of the sea floor, a team of Canadian scientists led by Daryl Fedje and Heiner Josenhans

identified old sites of ponds and lakes, riverbeds, tree stumps, pinecones, and twigs. When they dredged up mud and silt, they recovered bits of wood in it that were dated as 12,200 years old.

Researchers also identified three underwater landmasses between Queen Charlotte and Vancouver islands. Although these places are now beneath the water's surface, they would have stuck out as islands during part of the last ice age. Boat people could have made it from one island to the next as they explored their way down the coast.

These studies indicated that humans *could* have survived in the area 12,200 years ago and probably earlier than that. But *were* they there? Where was the evidence of humans?

By incredible luck, on May 17, 1998, one of the dredges brought up from the floor, about 170 feet below, a stone tool partly covered by barnacles! Was this the proof? Again, those tough rules of archaeology had to be applied. A single tool could have fallen from a passing boat at a later date. Until more evidence is found, we just cannot be sure.

Crossing an Ocean to South America?

Early humans reached Australia at least 40,000 years ago. Twenty-five thousand five hundred years later (14,500 years ago), someone from somewhere arrived at Monte Verde in South America. Could people have sailed across the South Pacific to get there?

When a boat left shore, how far could it move out to sea before the land behind it disappeared from sight? Sailors would have to see land ahead or risk becoming lost and perishing at sea.

Scientists have studied the possibility of this kind of ocean crossing by mapping the distance between islands that might have provided "stepping stones" across the South Pacific.

Charts show that stone-age sailors could have traveled great distances by keeping islands in sight. But there would be long stretches with no land on the horizon. Even if one lucky boat made it to South America, it's hard to imagine bringing enough people to start a population and keep it going.

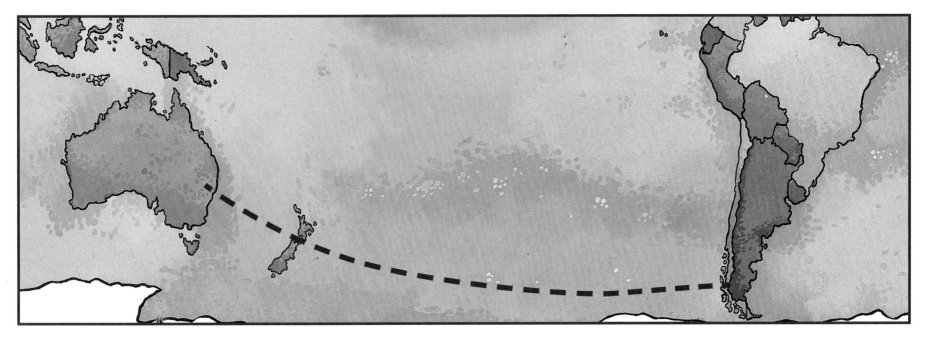

Could early humans have reached South America from Australia?

Was There a European Connection?

A people known as Solutreans (say-loo-TREE-ans) existed long before Clovis, from about twenty-five thousand to eighteen thousand years ago. Both Solutrean and Clovis stone points required controlled chipping, but Solutrean points weren't fluted and they tended to be leaf-shaped. On the other hand, both Solutrean and Clovis hunters chipped their points on both sides.

Some archaeologists have wondered if Solutreans could have been the inspiration for Clovis craftsmen who came along thousands of years later. However, not many scientists agree. Solutrean tool makers didn't come to the west of North America from Asia. They lived to the east, across the Atlantic Ocean. Evidence of Solutrean tool making has been discovered in France, Portugal, Spain, and southern England. To reach North America, they would have had a long, long way to go. As far as we know, Solutreans were not seafaring people. Could small groups of men, women, and children make it three thousand miles across the frigid North Atlantic during the peak of the ice age?

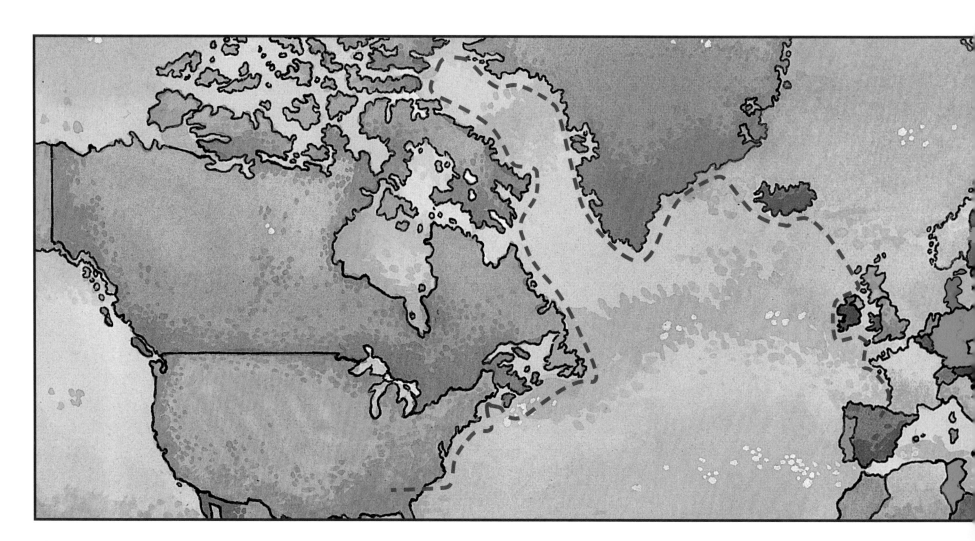

Possible Solutrean route from Europe to North America

Impossible Voyage?

It would have seemed suicidal to attempt crossing the open waters of the wild and cold North Atlantic. If for some reason the Solutreans decided to take to the ocean, their best bet would be to hug shorelines where they could seek shelter from storms and rough seas.

If they headed north past Ireland, they would eventually need to turn westward and pick their way along the enormous ice packs off Iceland and Greenland. Finally, they would have to turn south and move down the east coast of North America. Would this trip be long and miserable?

It would be long for sure, but maybe not always miserable. The coastlines would be rich in marine life, and the Solutreans were accustomed to making temporary shelters along the banks. Such a voyage might not have been so impossible after all.

Archaeologists who don't believe this happened say it is only a coincidence that people in Europe and North America had similar stone points and shared some other traits. By eighteen thousand years ago, so much water was frozen into gigantic glaciers that land along our east coast was exposed for up to 150 miles beyond today's shores. Traces of Solutrean sailors, if there were any, now lie underwater.

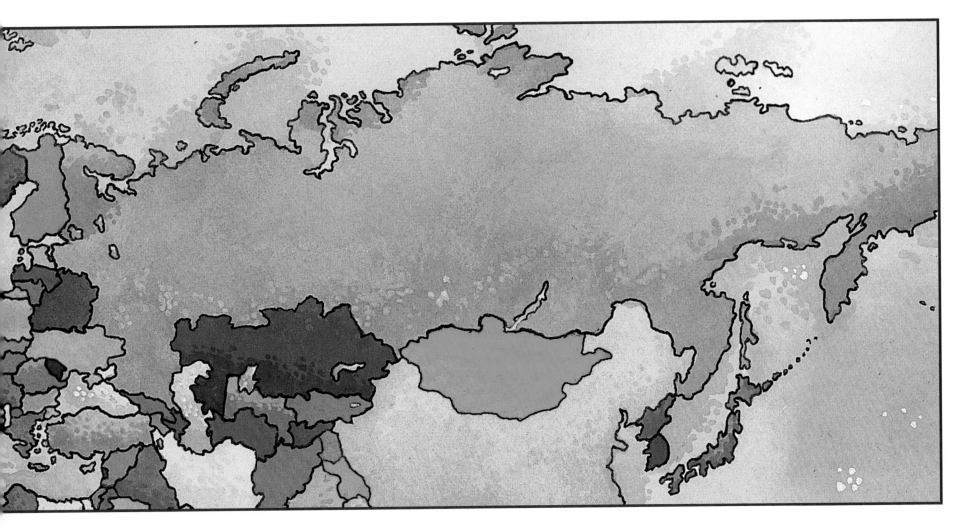

LOOKING IN AN ANCIENT MIRROR 8

Summing Up

ARCHAEOLOGISTS HAVE NOW UNCOVERED
millions of traces of our human history in North and South
America. More and more scientists around the world are involved
in the search.

We have learned a great deal about those early settlers.
Their brains were the size of ours. They spoke a language and
controlled fire. They gathered, picked, and dug. Early hunters
went after game of all sizes. They trapped and fished.

Their diet included a wide variety of plants and animals. They
used plants for medicine. They made clothes as well as moccasins
and boots, which protected their feet. They constructed shelters,
fashioned rope, and made a variety of baskets. Early craftsmen
created utensils, jewelry, needles, mats, bags, tools, and weapons
from a variety of materials.

Reading the Bones

Few human bones have been found to offer glimpses of our early ancestors. That far back, the total number of people on the continent would have been small, so unearthing even a single human bone fragment is exceedingly rare. With such a limited sample to study, scientists can't make many conclusions, but it seems clear that life could be harsh and brief.

Based on thirty-eight human findings, it appears that people then were shorter than we are now. The tallest man was 5 feet 9 inches. Next tallest was 5 feet 4 inches.

About three out of four children died before reaching adulthood. Most adults died in their twenties and thirties. One person in ten lived past forty, and only one person in the whole group of samples made it to fifty.

About one person in four died from injuries. People suffered from hunger and disease. Some had problems with their teeth and endured awful pain from abscesses and infections.

More Questions than Answers

As you read this book, archaeologists continue to learn more about our past. Vital missing links are out there—or down there—waiting to be found. They rest beneath desert sands or boggy swamp bottoms. They wait under riverbanks, cave debris, or silt on ocean floors. Somewhere a melting glacier is about to expose something (or someone) frozen since the last ice age. A core sample being winched onto a boat will hold evidence of an ancient flooded settlement.

Linguists (people who study languages) search for clues to our past by comparing languages spoken by Native Americans with those spoken by native groups in Asia, Europe, and other continents. Anatomists (those who study the human body) look for similarities in tooth development among native groups. Geneticists (scientists who study inherited traits) have found relationships between American Indian groups and native groups in Siberia, east Asia, and Europe.

As scattered pieces of this baffling puzzle are found, we gradually see the picture of our past more clearly. We may always have more questions than answers, and every answer creates new questions. The task is daunting but worth the trouble. Who were North America's first people? We still don't know. It may have taken thousands of years and wave after wave of new arrivals from different locations to finally settle here. Whether they came on foot or by boat, they came. Our quest goes on.

The quest goes on to uncover clues to our past.

Glossary

Anthropologist: Scientist who studies the development of human cultures.

Archaeologist: Scientist who studies past human life and cultures by recovering and examining remaining evidence.

Artifact: A man-made object from the past, such as scraps of clothing, pottery, and stone points.

Carbon-14: A carbon atom altered by cosmic rays to make a radioactive form that slowly deteriorates over time. Carbon is an abundant element in the human body and throughout the universe.

Clovis: An early group of people who arrived in North America about 13,125 years ago; a technique for making stone tools and weapons that developed around that time.

Clovis First: A theory that Clovis people were the first humans to arrive in North America.

Glacial: The proper term for the "ice ages" that come in cycles of about 100,000 years. True ice ages last millions of years. It is thought that there have been at least four ice ages in Earth's history.

Holocene: A period of geologic time, called an epoch. We are living in the Holocene Epoch, which began about 10,000 years ago.

Homo sapiens: We are *Homo sapiens*. Our ancestors came from Africa 200,000 years ago or more.

Ice ages: Commonly used interchangeably with *glacial* or *glacial age*. More accurately, it refers to the four or five extended periods in Earth's history when ice covered most of the planet.

Mammoth: Ancient relative of today's elephant that evolved about 4.8 million years ago. Most died out by 12,000 years ago, but some in isolated areas survived longer.

Mastodon: Resembled the mammoth but came from a different family. Both were about the same height and lived during much of the same time. Mastodons were browsers while mammoths were grazers.

Microblades: Sharp stone flakes inserted into a shaft to make a weapon or tool.

Pleistocene: A period of geologic time, called an epoch, that began roughly two million years ago and ended 10,000 years ago.

Pre-Clovis: Humans who may have arrived in North America before Clovis people.

Sandstone: Sand particles laid down in layers over time, pressed under great weight of layers of earth or sea water above, and cemented together by an active mineral such as quartz.

Solutrean: A technique for making stone tools and weapons created by people who lived in Europe approximately 25,000 to 18,000 years ago. Named after the site in eastern France where evidence was first discovered.

Sonar: A system of sending out underwater sound waves and measuring how long it takes echoes to bounce back from objects below.

Species: Scientific term to identify each living thing. The human species is *sapiens*. The black bear is *americanus* and the lion is *leo*.

Volcanic rock: Began as part of a volcano's molten lava flow or explosion and later cooled back into a new form of rock.

Photo Sources

Courtesy Neil Lopinot, **Center for Archaeological Research, Missouri State University**: 6 (bottom photo by Jack Ray); 26, 27, 45

Courtesy of Anthony T. Boldurin, **Clovis Archives**: 14, 16

Courtesy of **Joanne Dickenson**: 17 (left)

Courtesy of the **Gault Project, Texas Archaeological Research Laboratory, the University of Texas at Austin**: 22–23, photos by Sam Gardner; Department of Anthropology, Brigham Young University: 27 (right)

David L. Harrison: 17 (right)

Courtesy J. M. Adovasio, **Mercyhurst Archaeology Institute, Mercyhurst College**: 33, 34 (top left and right)

© **Juliet E. Morrow**, used with permission: 20 (top)

Courtesy of Al Goodyear, **South Carolina Institute for Archaeology and Anthropology, University of South Carolina**. Photo by Keith E. McGraw, Jr.: 34 (bottom)

Southeastern Paleoamerican Survey, Inc. (SEPAS, Inc.), Daryl P. Miller: 35

Courtesy Tom Dillehay, Department of Anthropology, **Vanderbilt University**: 30–32

Maps courtesy of Highlights for Children, Inc.

References

Adovasio, J. M. *The First Americans: In Pursuit of Archaeology's Greatest Mystery*. With Jake Page. New York: Random House, 2002.

Barton, Miles, et al. *Prehistoric America: A Journey through the Ice Age and Beyond*. New Haven, CT: Yale University Press, 2002.

Boldurian, Anthony T. "Hooking Students on Clovis." *Mammoth Trumpet*. (2004).

Boldurian, Anthony T. "Memorial, James Ridgley Whiteman, 1910–2003." *Plains Anthropologist* 49, no. 149 (2004).

Cannon, Michael D., and David J. Meltzer. "Early Paleoindian Foraging: Examining the Faunal Evidence for Large Mammal Specialization and Regional Variability in Prey Choice." *Quaternary Science Reviews* 23 (2004).

Cinq-Mars, Jacques. "The Significance of the Bluefish Caves in Beringian Prehistory." *Quebec Archaeological Survey of Canada* (2001).

Collins, Michael B. "The Gault Site, Texas, and Clovis Research." *Athena Review* 3, no. 2 (2002).

Cook, Joseph A., et al. "Beringia: Intercontinental Exchange and Diversification of High Latitude Mammals and Their Parasites during the Pliocene and Quaternary." *The Mammalogical Society of Japan* (2006).

Dalton, Rex. "Blast in the Past?" *Nature: International Weekly Journal of Science* 447 (May 17, 2007): 256–257.

Dillehay, Thomas D. *The Settlement of the Americas: A New Prehistory*. New York: Basic Books, 2000.

Dixon, E. James. *Bones, Boats, and Bison: Archaeology and the First Colonization of Western North America*. Albuquerque: University of New Mexico Press, 1999.

Fagan, Brian M. *Ancient North America*. 4th ed. New York: Thames and Hudson, 2005.

Goodyear, Albert C. "Evidence for Pre-Clovis Sites in the Eastern United States." In *Paleoamerican Origins: Beyond Clovis*, edited by Robson Bonnichsen, et al. College Station: Center for the Study of the First Americans, Texas A&M University Press, 2005.

Kirchweger, Gina. "The Biology of Skin Color: Black and White." *Discover* 22, no. 2 (February 2001).

Koppel, Tom. *Lost World: Rewriting Prehistory: How New Science Is Tracing America's Ice Age Mariners*. New York: Atria Books, 2003.

Lange, Ian M. *Ice Age Mammals of North America: A Guide to the Big, Hairy, and the Bizarre*. Missoula, MT: Mountain Press, 2002.

Lopinot, Neal H., Jack H. Ray, and Michael D. Conner. *The 1999 Excavations at the Big Eddy Site* (23CE426). Special Publication No. 3. Springfield: Center for Archaeological Research, Missouri State University, 2000.

Mehringer, Peter Joseph, Jr. "Weapons of Ancient Americans." *National Geographic*, October 1988.

Monastersky, R. "Drowned Land Holds Clue to First Americans." *Science News Online*, February 5, 2000.

Morrow, Juliet E. "A Clovis Camp at the Martens Site." *Arkansas Archaeological Survey*. Jonesboro: Arkansas State University, 2000.

Pielou, E. C. *After the Ice Age: The Return of Life to Glaciated North America*. Chicago: University of Chicago Press, 1991.

Rozell, Ned. "Searching for Ancient Answers in Southeast Alaska." Address, Alaska Science Forum, provided by the Geophysical Institute, University of Alaska, Fairbanks, May 29, 2003.

Stone, Richard. *Mammoth: The Resurrection of an Ice Age Giant*. Cambridge, MA: Perseus Publishing, 2001.

Turk, Jon. *In the Wake of Jomon: Stone Age Mariners and a Voyage across the Pacific*. Camden, ME: International Marine / McGraw-Hill, 2005.

Waters, Michael R., and Thomas W. Stafford Jr. "Redefining the Age of Clovis: Implications for the Peopling of the Americas." *Science* 315 (February 23, 2007).

INDEX

Italicized page numbers refer to captions, photographs, and illustrations.

Text copyright © 2010 by David L. Harrison
Illustrations copyright © 2010 by Richard Hilliard

Boyds Mills Press, Inc.
815 Church Street
Honesdale, Pennsylvania 18431
Printed in the United States of America

First edition
10 9 8 7 6 5 4 3 2 1

Library of Congress Cataloging-in-Publication Data

Harrison, David L.
    Mammoth bones and broken stones : the mystery of North America's first people / David L. Harrison ; with Illustrations by Richard Hilliard and archaeological photographs. — 1st ed.
        p. cm.
    Includes bibliographical references and index.
    ISBN 978-1-59078-561-4 (hardcover : alk. paper)
    1. Paleo-Indians—Juvenile literature. 2. North America—Antiquities—Juvenile literature. I. Hilliard, Richard. II. Title.
    E61.H28 2010
    970.01—dc22

                    2009020247